CONNECTED©

By

Craig Christie

FOR ALL ENQUIRIES CONTACT: ORiGiN™ Theatrical
PO BOX Q1235, QVB Post Office, Sydney, NSW, 1230, Australia
Phone: (61 2) 8514 5201 Fax: (61 2) 9299 2920
enquiries@originmusic.com.au   www.origintheatrical.com.au
Part of the ORiGiN™ Music Group
An Australian Independent Music Company

IMPORTANT NOTICE

First Published © 2013 ORiGiN™ Theatical
Reprinted 2015. School Edition.

The amateur and professional acting rights to this work are controlled exclusively by ORiGiN™ Theatrical (the publisher). Permission in writing is required by ORiGiN™ Theatrical, or their agent, before a performance is given. A performance is given any time it is acted before an audience. A royalty fee is payable before each and every performance regardless of whether it is for a non-profit organisation or if an admission is charged.

The publication of this play does not mean that the amateur and professional performance rights are available. It is highly recommended that you apply for performance rights before starting rehearsals and/or booking rehearsal or performance spaces.

Visit the ORiGiN™ Theatrical website for applications and information www.origintheatrical.com.au or address your inquiry to ORiGiN™ Theatrical, PO Box Q1235, QVB Post Office, Sydney, NSW 1230, Australia.

This work is fully protected by copyright. No alterations, substitutions or deletions can be made to this work without the prior consent of the publisher. It is expressly prohibited to broadcast, televise, film, videotape, record, translate or transmit to subscribers through a diffusion service that currently exists or is yet to be invented, this work or any portion thereof whatsoever without permission in writing from the publisher.

Copying or reproducing, without permission, of all or any part of this book, in any form, is an infringement of copyright.

Copyright provides the creators with an incentive to invest their time, talent and other resources to create new works. Authors earn their living from the royalties they receive from book sales and from the performance of the work. Copyright law provides a legal framework for control of their creations.

Whenever this play is produced, the billing and credit requirements *must* appear on all programs distributed in connection with the performance and in all instances in which the title of the play appears for the purposes of advertising, seeking publicity for the play or otherwise exploiting the play and/or a performance(s).

While this play may contain references to brand names or trademarks owned by third parties, or make reference to public figures, ORiGiN™ Theatrical should not be considered to be necessarily endorsing or otherwise attempting to promote an affiliation with any of the owners of the brand names or trademarks of public figures. Such references are solely for use in a dramatic context.

If you are in any doubt about any of the above then contact ORiGiN™ Theatrical.

LANGUAGE NOTE

Licensees are welcome to make small alterations to the language that is used is this play so as to make it suitable for a younger cast and/or audience.

www.origintheatrical.com.au

AND HERE ARE THE RULES IN PLAIN ENGLISH FOR YOU...

DO NOT perform this play without getting permission from ORiGiN™ Theatrical first. In 99% of cases you'll need to pay us money to be allowed to stage a performance. This money goes to the author(s) of the show who shed blood, sweat and tears creating this play. Please don't rob them of their livelihood.
Go online www.origintheatrical.com.au or call +61 2 8514 5201

DO NOT make a copy of this book by photocopying, scanning, taking a photo, retyping (on a computer or a typewriter), or using a pencil, pen or chalkboard. If you want to purchase more copies contact ORiGiN™ Theatrical.
Go online www.origintheatrical.com.au or call +61 2 8514 5201

DO NOT make any changes to the text without first getting permission from ORiGiN™ Theatrical in writing. Sometimes you'll be allowed to make changes and sometimes you won't. Please always check with us first.
Go online www.origintheatrical.com.au or call +61 2 8514 5201

DO NOT record your performances or rehearsals in anyway without first getting permission from ORiGiN™ Theatrical. We know everyone wants to try and record everything on their phones these days. We get it. But please don't encourage them or give them permission. Sometimes there are important contractual reasons as to why we can't give you permission to record it. And sometimes there aren't any reasons and we can say YES. Please just check with us first.
Go online www.origintheatrical.com.au or call +61 2 8514 5201

DO contact ORiGiN™ Theatrical if you have any questions about anything. At all. And we mean anything. One of us that works here (not me) has a peculiar interest in recording the unusual bird calls of the adult hoatzin (a species of tropical bird found in wet forest and mangrove of the Amazon and the Orinoco delta in South America) so we should be able to answer any questions you have about the Hoatzin. Plus we know some things about some other things too.

Thank you for taking the time to read this.

by the same author

Jungle Bungle

Rev It Up!

Eurobeat: Moldova

The Web, Wires & Waves

You See What Really Happens Is…

Ice

Losing My Patients

One Night

Snow White and the Seven Sins

Hush

Fifteen Minutes of Fame

The Great Pretender

Christmas Turkey

My Friends Dot Com

Craig Christie Songbook

Foreword

Following recent media coverage of teenage suicides in Australia and the United States, the phenomenon of cyber bullying has risen dramatically in the public consciousness. When a young person suicides in the prime of their life the impact on family, friends, school and the wider community is profound. Intense hurt, anger and disbelief drives a shared focus on trying to understand why this tragedy has occurred in the hope that it might be prevented from happening again in the future.

Moreover, suicide is not the only concern related to cyber bullying. Research has found that one in five students in Australia are cyber bullied and that the detrimental effects on health are at least as bad as that of traditional bullying. We know that students who are bullied suffer from higher rates of depression, anxiety, low self esteem, reduced concentration and helplessness.

So what does cyber bullying look like? Cyberbullying is *"wilful & repeated harm inflicted through the medium of electronic text"* (Patchin & Hinduja, 2006). Bullying of this nature can manifest in wide and varied forms such as offensive, derogatory or threatening messages sent via text, instant messages, email, computer games, school websites, youtube, social networking sites (e.g., Bebo, Myspace, Facebook), blogs, chat sites and bulletin boards. Embarrassing or elicit pictures might be posted on websites, or sent via email, mobiles or text. Emails, texts or photos are being forwarded without consent. As we see in the following script, damaging rumours can be spread like wildfire online. Viruses and security attacks can also be used to cyber bully by erasing someone's hard drive or stealing their identity. Indeed, the cyber bully's methods are limited only by their technical expertise and creativity.

Are cyberbullies just traditional schoolyard bullies with access to computers and mobile phones? The answer to this is yes and no. There is a large overlap between the two groups of bullies. Many young people who bully in the schoolyard also do so online.

However, there is a substantial group of young people who engage in bullying online who have never bullied anyone else in the traditional sense. Thus, technology has created a whole new breed of bullies who would not have otherwise engaged in this harmful activity.

This brings us to the unique features of cyber bullying many of which are artfully illustrated in the following dramatic script. Most people who are cyber bullied do not know who their bully is which can lead to feelings of fear and paranoia as they confront the outside world. Imagine arriving at school after receiving abusive emails not knowing if 1 or 100 students are involved and even what has prompted the emails. The anonymity afforded the cyber bully enables them to be disinhibited and to act in ways they wouldn't ordinarily act in real life. Sitting behind a screen, the bully doesn't see the hurt inflicted on the other party and is therefore unlikely to feel empathy that might serve to modify their destructive behavior.

Cyber bullies often minimize their behavior, just as the characters in this play do with regularity. "It's not real, we're just having some fun, it's just teasing" are common excuses. The reasons that people cyber bully are variable, as this script will attest. Interestingly, research tells us that many cyber bullies engage in cyber bullying simply because they are bored. On the other hand, others may be out to "right a wrong" or to put somebody in their place.

The cyber community is constant; 24/7 around the clock. As long as the bullied person is online they exist in an inescapable hostile environment. It's not as simple as turning the technology off as this is akin to social suicide for these generations; they live and breathe through social media. The norm for young people is to conduct their social lives through an electronic medium. Unfortunately though, this leaves them open to a toxic environment of abuse at all hours. What's more, in contrast to traditional bullying whereby a student is bullied in front of a group in the schoolyard, online bullying can occur in front of an entire school community, a national or even international audience. Within seconds images can be uploaded and distributed to very large numbers of recipients.

Many cyber bullies, particularly girls, cyber bully in groups. Thus cyber bullying is often a spectator sport which holds a clue as to possible interventions. We know that bullying - schoolyard or digital - often takes place in a context whereby other students stand by (or observe), watch the bullying and do not intervene. Many schools now are training students in bystander intervention so students are equipped with the skills to stand up and say something to put a stop to bullying.

This play is written for young people, and acted by young people, to highlight how small, seemingly frivolous actions, can translate into devastating effects on the person being cyber bullied. It implores the viewer to consider their role as a bystander or bully and the flow on effects that can be a result of their actions. We are navigating our way in a world that is changing the very way that we relate to each other. Ultimately this play seeks to generate discussion about the social mores of this new and exciting electronic world.

Dr Rachael Murrihy
Senior Clinical Psychologist
Health Psychology Unit
University of Technology Sydney
New South Wales
Australia

Introduction

It crept up on me. I had heard stories, read some in the papers or circulated online and then there was an incident involving the daughter of a friend of mine. Even so I was unprepared for how profound and serious the problem of cyber bullying was until I decided to explore the issue to prepare writing a short show to tour into primary schools. I was horrified as incident after incident outlined the pain inflicted upon the helpless, the misery caused by the cruelty of faceless cowards, the thoughtlessness and ignorance of those who ought to be caring and protecting and the tragic consequences. And all this was occurring constantly, insidiously as people young and old struggled along day after day in fear of what might be being said or circulated about them.

Initially I wrote a show called *My Friends Dot Com* which exposed this and brought it forward as a springboard for discussion in the classroom for primary school students (and I have to add I was astonished and appalled to find out how young the perpetrators and victims of cyber bullying can be). However the constraints of time and audience meant that I didn't have the opportunity to fully explore characters and the evolution of situations involved in the plot. Hence I decided to write a full length version of the show so I could explore the relationships between the characters, the rationalisation of some of them, the suffering of others and the far reaching consequences for everyone involved. This became *Connected*. In publishing it there were constraints upon the language and actions because of the context – school – that this script is likely to be used in but I am sure that people who read and act the script and audience members can create their own vocabulary to make the dialogue ring more truly. I also chose the form of a musical to tell the story as songs have the ability to distil moments, express eloquently the inarticulate speech of the heart and to grab attention and engage the audience.

Finally despite the headlines that occur and the stories that are circulated, the reality and occurrence of cyber bullying has not diminished. This script and the story it presents remains frighteningly relevant. Hopefully it will engage readers, performers and audiences in the characters and the situations that unfold in the narrative and in doing so will make some impact in teaching people everywhere how to be kinder and more responsible cyber citizens.

Craig Christie

"I thought the show was fantastic and very relevant! It is SO important that children are educated about this issue."
Wahroonga Adventist School

"The students were shocked by some aspects of cyber bullying."
Collingwood College

"The show is great as it covers real life issues, and the music and the performances were FANTASTIC!"
Bacchus Marsh College

"Great performance. Funny, engaging and educational way of presenting the dangers and repercussions of not thinking about how online actions affect others! Well Done!"
Parkwood Green PS

"Great performance. A very powerful presentation that hopefully will help keep our students safe from harm."
Fawkner PS

"Kids loved the show and found it very relatable. Gave a great awareness into Cyber Safety."
Otahuhu Primary School, Auckland 2011

"Loved that it was related to real issues, and the humour was spot on! A very important message was expressed to the students and has provided wonderful opportunities for follow up work and discussion."
Karaka School, Auckland 2011

"The children were very focused and engaged the whole time."
Muritai School, Wellington 2011

CONNECTED©

By Craig Christie

CHARACTERS

DYLAN – A computer nerd. Shy and socially inept.
KATE – Popular, egocentric and manipulative.
EMMA – The new girl. Uncertain and vulnerable.
MICHAEL – School jock. Nice guy but not that smart.
Voice of DYLAN'S Mum / Voice of MADDY

The story is set in and around the school yard and in the bedrooms of Dylan and Emma.

SONGS

1. Connected – Dylan, Kate, Emma and Michael
2. Planet Kate – Michael
3. 184 Friends (Parts 1, 2 & 3) – Emma
4. Gotta Do – Kate
5. Oh Nothing – Dylan and Emma
6. Somebody Else – Dylan
7. Got To Stop – Michael
8. Easy Way Out – Emma
9. Don't Ask Me – Dylan, Kate and Michael
10. Connected (reprise) – Dylan, Kate, Emma and Michael

DYLAN IS IN HIS ROOM AT HIS COMPUTER WHEN HE STARTS TAPPING A KEY REPEATEDLY.

DYLAN: Oh damn! No, no, no!

CONNECTED

DYLAN: I just got disconnected
When I was about to see
This sick new game from Europe
Someone sent the link to me
Can't go to school tomorrow
Because I don't want to be
The only guy who looks as if he doesn't know what's going on

KATE: I just ran out of charge as
I was reading Rachel's text
I know that Dan arrived but
I don't know what happened next
She'll think that I'm ignoring her
Coz that's what she expects
I hate it when I can't find out just what the hell is going on

TOGETHER: You've got to be connected
You've got to know what's in and what is out
You've got to stay connected
The only way to know what life's about
It don't take much to have it
Or to have it ripped away
Coz that's what's needed to be popular
Just be connected

EMMA: I heard about some crazy girl who lived in Tennessee
She said that she would kill herself and stream it publicly
Nobody tried to stop her coz they all wanted to see
She's been a guest on Ellen and is now a star on MTV

MICHAEL: A mate filmed me a while back sticking pencils up my nose
I posted it on YouTube, I was joking I suppose
It's now had forty million hits and everybody knows
The pencil guy from Melbourne who's more popular than One Direction

ALL: You've got to be connected
You've got to know what's in and what is out
You've got to stay connected
The only way to know what life's about
It don't take much to have it
Or to have it ripped away
Coz that's what's needed to be popular
Just be connected

If you've read something online well then it must be true
If someone heard it somewhere then it must be true
If it is on a website then it must be true
If you think that perhaps maybe then it must be true

If it was texted to you then it must be true
If everyone is Tweeting it, it must be true
If it's up on someone's Facebook then it must be true
If you believe it there's no doubt it must be true

EMMA: Hi. I'm Emma. My family has just moved to Sydney from up in Moree. I don't know anyone here but I'm looking forward to making some new friends.

DYLAN: My name's Dylan but if you're like most people you're not really interested.

KATE: I'm Kate but most of you would already know that because I'm one of those people who everyone knows and everyone wants to be friends with. I get on well with just about everyone. I'm even nice to losers and geeks.

MICHAEL: Michael. (winks and gives a thumbs up sign)

> ALL: You gotta be connected
> You've got to know what's in and what is out
> You've got to stay connected
> The only way to know what life's about
> It don't take much to have it
> Or to have it ripped away
> Coz that's what's needed to be popular
> Just be connected.

* * * * *

EMMA WALKS UP TO MICHAEL.

EMMA: Hi. Could you help me for a second?

MICHAEL: Huh?

EMMA: I'm in your English class. It's my first day. I don't remember what book we have to read.

MICHAEL: Don't worry about it. You're new. I reckon that gives you a few weeks to do nothing if you don't want to. The teachers will just think you're just 'adjusting'.

EMMA: Don't worry about it. SHE GOES TO LEAVE.

MICHAEL: What's your number?

EMMA: What?

MICHAEL: Your number. I'll text it to you.

EMMA: I don't even know your name.

MICHAEL: That's okay. I don't know yours.

EMMA: It's Emma.

MICHAEL: Okay Emma. Give me your mobile number and I'll text the name of the book to you when I remember what it is.

EMMA: It's fine. I can find out from the teacher.

MICHAEL: Suit yourself.

EMMA: You didn't tell me your name.

MICHAEL: Mike.

EMMA: See you in class I guess Mike. SHE EXITS.

MICHAEL: Well someone's up themselves. ENTER KATE.

KATE: That was quick work.

MICHAEL: What was?

KATE: I saw you chatting up the new girl just now. Are you sure she's your type?

MICHAEL: I'm sure she's not. Weird. First day here and she is spending time worrying about school work and just ignoring me when I'm trying to be friendly.

KATE: What do you mean 'trying to be friendly'?

MICHAEL: I was just trying to help her out.

KATE: So you DO like her then.

MICHAEL: I told you I was just trying to be friendly. How was I supposed to know she had issues?

KATE: She'd better watch out. People don't like it when a new girl comes in and starts showing interest in guys without even checking if they might be in a relationship.

MICHAEL: A relationship? With who? With you? Kate you dumped me.

KATE: Get over yourself. And don't say it like that. It sounds as if it was all my fault and I explained to you why.

MICHAEL: I don't get you. Never did I guess.

KATE: I don't blame you for anything. But I think you should act sad about it a bit longer before you chat up every new girl who walks into the school.

MICHAEL: For God's sake I wasn't chatting her up.

KATE: Doesn't matter. There are rules and she needs to learn them.

MICHAEL: I don't care what you do. She didn't even want to give me her number so I could help her out. I wouldn't call that a pick up.

KATE: Playing hard to get is the oldest trick in the book.

MICHAEL: Maybe that's why it doesn't work.

KATE: If you're referring to me in any way I thought I made it clear why I had to break up with you Mike.

MICHAEL: You expect me to buy that rubbish about your horoscope and keeping yourself free for opportunities.

KATE: Obviously you're too immature to understand. I sent you the link to explain it. Did you even bother to look at it?

MICHAEL: A link. You break up with me and send me a link to a horoscope website and expect me to say "hey that's cool. I accept that".

KATE: The horoscope just pointed out what I had been feeling anyway Mike. It's not the right time for me to limit myself with my relationships. The wrong choice now could ruin my life.

MICHAEL: Why are you so sure I'm the wrong choice though?

KATE: You want me to take that chance?

MICHAEL: Come on Kate. Remember that time when you thought the world was going to explode because of the Mayan calendar? You need to stop getting sucked in by that crap.

KATE: One thing I'm not going to be sucked in by is you.

PLANET KATE

MICHAEL: You're pathetic and you know it
You are gonna fall flat on your face
It's just crazy and you'll blow it
Then you'll disappear without a trace.
Look at me I'm real I'm here and asking you to come back to your senses
Don't forget the good things that we have.

You're a dreamer yeah I get that
And you're wanting something to believe
But it makes me want to throw up
Sweetheart how can you be so naïve?
Buy your magazines and watch your crap TV if that stuff makes you happy
But remember none of it is real.

Oh this is Mike to Planet Kate
It's time you came back down to Earth
Sure I know the view is great
But let me tell you what it's worth.
It's nothing. It's nothing. It's nothing
You'll soon have nothing at all.

SHE TURNS TO LEAVE. HE BLOCKS HER.

MICHAEL: Oh Kate.

KATE: What?

MICHAEL: Just hear me out.

> Look you hurt me. I forgive you
> If you promise you will pack it in
> I'll pretend it never happened
> But the joke is wearing pretty thin
> What's your problem? Tell me honestly what's wrong with living in the real world
> It can get lonely there in outer space

KATE ROLLS HER EYES AND EXITS.

> Oh this is Mike to Planet Kate
> It's time you came back down to Earth
> Sure I know the view is great
> But let me tell you what it's worth.
> It's nothing. It's nothing. It's nothing
> You'll soon have nothing

HE STARTS TEXTING HER.

> No-one to hide your face on at the scary parts in movies
> No-one to cry to when you fight with your Dad
> No-one you can rely on to be patient when you go out shopping
> Nobody who loves you
> No-one who doesn't think you're barking mad
>
> Oh this is Mike to Planet Kate
> It's time you came back down to Earth

Sure I know the view is great
But let me tell you what it's worth

KATE RE-ENTERS WAVING HER PHONE HAVING READ HIS TEXT.

I am calling Planet Kate
Hey, is there anybody home?
The lights are on but no-one answers
Come back from the twilight zone
There's nothing. It's nothing. You're nothing.

KATE: Can I go now? SHE TURNS TO LEAVE. ENTER DYLAN.

DYLAN: Hi Kate.

KATE: Bye Dylan. SHE EXITS.

DYLAN: CALLING AFTER HER. Did you see my post about that band you wanted to go see? PAUSE. Guess she's busy.

MICHAEL: Ooh crash and burn.

DYLAN: Well it doesn't matter is she hasn't got time to talk to me now. I can talk to her online tonight. She'll need to catch me at the right time though. She hasn't got nearly as many friends as I have on Facebook and I can get really busy if a whole lot of them are online at the same time.

MICHAEL: And you think that's an achievement? Keep telling yourself that. MICHAEL EXITS.

DYLAN: CALLING AFTER HIM. Maybe people in this crappy school don't think I'm cool but I've got friends all over the world.

HE STANDS THERE AWKWARDLY. EMMA ENTERS AT A DISTANCE. THEY EYE EACH OTHER SELF CONSCIOUSLY UNTIL FINALLY EMMA BREAKS THE TENSION AND MOVES ACROSS.

EMMA: Hey I'm looking for the office. Could you just point me in the right direction? I seem to have walked right around the whole school in a big circle.

DYLAN: Umm sure. Look it's just in the next block, you take the second doorway down and… How about I just show you.

EMMA: Thanks.

DYLAN: New huh?

EMMA: Yep. First day.

DYLAN: How's it going?

EMMA: Ok.

DYLAN: Cool. THEY WALK A BIT. DYLAN SUMMONS HIS COURAGE. So what's your name?

EMMA: Emma. AWKWARD PAUSE.

DYLAN: Dylan. What year?

EMMA: Eleven.

DYLAN: Me too. ANOTHER PAUSE. Umm just down there. See the second door.

EMMA: Cool thanks… Dylan.

DYLAN: Cool. HE STANDS FOR A MOMENT. Okay. Bye. HE EXITS.

184 FRIENDS - PART ONE

EMMA: Well this is awkward
Well this is not how things should be
I'm not six, I'm sixteen
Yet here I am not sure how to move forward
What's the best way to settle in?
I don't know anyone
And I don't want to stuff things up before I have begun
But then I look at my phone and see
I've got 184 friends, big deal
I've got 184 friends
Not one of my 184 friends
Can help me in this situation
Make sense of this new location
There's no point in communication with
All of my 184 friends if they're not here.

* * * * *

DYLAN COMES HOME FROM SCHOOL AND GOES TO HIS ROOM.

VOICE OF MUM: Dylan. Is that you?

DYLAN: Yeah Mum.

VOICE OF MUM: Well you could at least say hello and let me know you're home.

DYLAN: Hello. I'm home.

VOICE OF MUM: Do you want a drink?

DYLAN: No I'm... I've got homework to do. PAUSE. HE GOES TO HIS COMPUTER AND LOGS ON.

VOICE OF MUM: You better not be wasting time on that computer.

DYLAN: CALLS. I've got to do my homework somehow. Do you want me to write it on the bedroom wall with a crayon?

VOICE OF MUM: Just don't spend the next two hours on Faceprint.

DYLAN: Real funny. HE FOCUSSES ON THE SCREEN. Let's see. Emma... Emma... Emma Williams. That's her. Request.

* * * * *

KATE IS ONSTAGE AS EMMA ENTERS.

KATE: Hi. Emma isn't it? I'm Kate.

EMMA: Hi.

KATE: What school did you come from?

EMMA: I was at Moree College. We just moved down to Sydney a week ago.

KATE: You seem to have made a bit of an impression already.

EMMA: Seriously? With who?

KATE: Oh I just heard a few people talking about you.

EMMA: But I only got here yesterday.

KATE: Oh you know how everyone is interested when a new person arrives.

EMMA: I guess so.

KATE: You'll be fine. You'll love being here. For starters there's so much more to do. You must have been bored out of your brain living up there. It would kill me being stuck in the middle of nowhere.

EMMA: It wasn't the middle of nowhere. And there was plenty to do. I mean maybe not the same shops and stuff but you wouldn't catch me or my friends saying "I'm bored".

KATE: Did you have a boyfriend?

EMMA: No-one special. As in boyfriend.

KATE: Well it's a whole new start now you're here. Nobody knows you so you can be a totally new person. Just be careful who you talk to and make friends with these first few days.

EMMA: Okay… Um thanks.

KATE: Just being friendly. See ya. KATE EXITS.

184 FRIENDS – PART TWO

EMMA: Well that's confusing
So what am I supposed to do?
Let her make up my mind
Or find out for myself. I should be using
My common sense at times like this
I should tread carefully
Until I understand the rules of popularity
Despite the fact when I'm online
I've got 184 friends, big deal…

ENTER DYLAN.

DYLAN: I friended you last night. Dylan. Remember?

EMMA: Oh yeah. Hi.

DYLAN: Must be tough having to start at a new school not knowing anyone.

EMMA: You have no idea. DYLAN SEARCHES FOR SOMETHING TO SAY BUT HAS NOTHING.

DYLAN: Okay then. WALKS OFF.

MICHAL HAS BEEN WATCHING HER AND DYLAN.

MICHAEL: Made a friend already I see?

EMMA: Huh?

MICHAEL: Dropkick Dylan. He your new BFF?

EMMA: I barely know him.

MICHAEL: I don't get you. You wouldn't give me your number yesterday when I just wanted to help you out and the next day you're friends with every loser in the school.

EMMA: It's not like that.

MICHAEL: Whatever.

EMMA: Look I'm new. I'm just trying to find my way around and settle in.

MICHAEL: And I'm just trying to help you.

184 FRIENDS – PART THREE

MICHAEL: You really should take my advice.

EMMA: Thanks but I'm okay.

KATE: I am only trying to be nice.

EMMA: Just trying to find my way.

DYLAN: Everyone has got their eyes on you.

DYLAN, KATE AND MICHAEL: Waiting to see what you'll do.

EMMA: I've got 184 friends… no wait
I've got 185 friends

MICHAEL: Big deal.

EMMA: I've got 186 friends

MICHAEL AND KATE: Big deal.

EMMA: I've got 187 friends.

MICHAEL, KATE AND DYLAN: Big deal.

DYLAN: I've got 1,973 friends…

MICHAEL GOES UP TO TALK TO KATE.

MICHAEL: You won't believe this. Dylan is all friends with the new chick. And when I spoke to her yesterday she wouldn't even give her number! So she's too good for me and then goes and bes friends with that noodle.

KATE: Don't stress. If she wants to join loserland let her. It sounds like that's where she belongs anyway.

MICHAEL: I just think she doesn't know what's good for her yet. Maybe we should try and save her before it's too late.

KATE: Save her from what? If she's a nerd it's in her DNA. You can't alter genetics.

MICHAEL: I suppose the next thing you're going to tell me it's probably her star sign.

KATE: Don't start.

MICHAEL: Start what?

KATE: You can laugh but my horoscope…

MICHAEL: You believing that crap shows how stupid you can be sometimes.

KATE: Stupid? What was stupid was the fact I stayed with you for so long.

MICHAEL: Why do you think that everything I have to say has something to do with us?

KATE: There is no us.

MICHAEL: I know. You and the stars made sure of that.

KATE: You know what. Just deal with it. Us getting back together is never going to happen.

MICHAEL: What makes you think I even want to get back with you? Plenty of options.

KATE: Like what? Like the new girl? LAUGHS. Go for it Mike. She's all yours.

MICHAEL: Maybe I will.

KATE: Just try it Mikey. It would be social suicide.

MICHAEL: Not that I need your permission but maybe someone who is actually nice is what I need.

KATE: Grow up Michael. Nice has nothing to do with it. You are such an Aries. It was never going to work. And remember - everyone has their place. Don't try and mess with things.

MICHAEL: Why don't you just go and find your star lover Kate. Think I'll look for something more down to earth. HE EXITS.

GOTTA DO

KATE: There must always be someone to show the world the way things are
It's a tough job someone's gotta do when they are popular
I didn't make up the rules
But when you're stuck with the fools
Who need direction then my path is clear

Sometimes I just gotta do what I gotta do
They can't see how hard it is but it's hard being perfect
Sometimes I just gotta be what I gotta be
Someone's gotta take the lead, gotta show the way to
Keep the order so that everybody knows their place

I know how to sort it out so I'll sort it out
I know that it may be harsh but there's no getting round it
I know who is number one and I'm number one
Gotta follow all the rules and the rules say that you need to know
Your place and who to look to for advice.

Spoken: Ok. Time to fix this mess out. PULLS OUT HER PHONE AND STARTS TEXTING. 'This is a skank alert. Watch out for new girl Emma. Only just got here and she's already got her eye on every guy in the school. Hashtag – Lock up your boyfriends'. There. That ought to sort it.

Sometimes I just gotta do what I gotta do
Someone's gotta take the lead so things all stay in order
Sometimes I just gotta be what I gotta be

Look I didn't make the rules, but the rules are there
It's not my fault if someone's hurt while I am going through
What I gotta do.

* * * * *

EMMA IS SITTING ALONE LOOKING MISERABLE. DYLAN ENTERS.

DYLAN: Hi Emma. What you got next period?

EMMA: Not sure. They still haven't given me a timetable.

DYLAN: You want me to go find out?

EMMA: If you want. Actually I think I might go home. I don't feel very well.

DYLAN: What's wrong?

EMMA: Nothing's wrong. I just… this place sucks.

DYLAN: What makes you say that?

EMMA: Look I went to ask a couple of people from my class what we had after lunch and they just abused me. And I don't even know them.

DYLAN: There are some pretty stupid people at this place.

EMMA: They said they knew all about me from my last school.

DYLAN: What did you do at your last school?

EMMA: Nothing. I didn't do anything. Just ordinary stuff. I don't know what they are talking about.

DYLAN: Maybe you're just being oversensitive.

EMMA: So you think I shouldn't be upset if I'm called all kinds of horrible things by two girls I don't even know.

DYLAN: If people are being like that to you maybe you should report it.

EMMA: I can't do that. That will just make things worse.

DYLAN: Yeah I guess so. Best ignore it. That's what I do. They'll get bored with it real quickly and leave you alone after that.

EMMA: I wish I'd never come to this school. I hate that my Dad was posted here. I wish I could just go back.

DYLAN: Hey don't let those wannabe mean girls turn you off this place. It's not bad here really. Well I don't think it's worse than anywhere else.

EMMA: You reckon?

DYLAN: Hey look. Why don't we just go and see what you've got after lunch. And if you want I can walk you home after school. They tend not to pick on people so much when you're not alone. Believe me I know all about it.

EMMA: You don't have to do that Dylan.

DYLAN: Oh ok. Hey I was just…

EMMA: No I'm not… I mean… Look I'll think about it.

DYLAN: DEFEATED. Never mind. HE GOES TO LEAVE.

EMMA: Look give me your number. I'll text you at the end of the day if things aren't any better.

DYLAN: You sure?

EMMA: TAKING OUT HER PHONE. Here just put your number into my contacts. HE DOES AND HANDS THE PHONE BACK.

DYLAN: There you go.

EMMA: Cool. Thanks Dylan.

DYLAN: Come on then. Lunchtime's almost over. POINTS. The Head of Year's office is down there. I've got to finish off some Biology in the Library. I'm going POINTING ANOTHER DIRECTION that way.

EMMA: Wait a sec. SHE PRESSES A BUTTON ON HER PHONE. DYLAN PAUSES AND THEN PULLS HIS PHONE OUT OF HIS POCKET. HE READS A TEXT MESSAGE.

DYLAN: 'Just checking'

EMMA: Yeah I just wanted to… Oh look anyway. You better go. THEY STAND THERE UNCERTAINLY.

OH NOTHING

DYLAN: Hey Emma?

EMMA: Yeah?

DYLAN: Oh nothing.

EMMA: Hey Dylan?

DYLAN: Yeah?

EMMA: Oh nothing.

TOGETHER: Hey Emma/Dylan? You first. It's not important.

DYLAN: I was just wondering what you were thinking about doing that thing that we were just talking about. That's all.

EMMA: I was just thinking you maybe were wondering What I thought about that thing we were talking about. That's all.

TOGETHER: So really it's nothing. Except maybe. Oh nothing. See you later.

DYLAN: If I was chilled or smart
Then this would be the part
Where I'd say something clever and she'd stay
But instead of being cool
I stand here like a fool
And watch her as she turns and walks away
So I'd better say

Emma

EMMA: Yeah?

DYLAN: Just wondered.

EMMA: What is it you wondered?

DYLAN: I wondered what you were going to say.

EMMA: Oh it's not important.

DYLAN: It might be important.

EMMA: I think that I've forgotten anyway.

DYLAN: Okay.

TOGETHER: I think there's something going on
But I'm scared. What if I was wrong?
Don't make a fool here of yourself
Just shut up and stay safe and lonely on the shelf.

DYLAN: Ok then.

EMMA: Ok then.

DYLAN: No worries.

EMMA: I'll see you.

DYLAN: I'll see you.

EMMA: No worries.

TOGETHER: It's been nice chatting. Guess I'll see you later.

DYLAN: Oh Emma?

EMMA: Yeah?

DYLAN: Oh nothing.

EMMA: Hey Dylan?

DYLAN: Yeah?

EMMA: Oh nothing.

TOGETHER: It sounds as if we needed a translator
I feel that there is something I should say
Bet I'll remember what it is soon as you walk away

EMMA EXITS. KATE INTERCEPTS DYLAN.

KATE: Hi Dylan. Made a new friend I see.

DYLAN: She is so cool.

KATE: Haven't you heard what everyone's been saying about her?

DYLAN: I don't know why people are saying such rubbish things after one day. They don't know her.

KATE: I heard that someone here is friends with someone from her old school who was told all about her last night on Skype. Didn't you see Claire's post?

DYLAN: I didn't see anything. Whatever people are saying I reckon it's all just lies.

KATE: Ooh got a crush on her have we?

DYLAN: It's not like that. We're just friends.

KATE: So what was going on with you two just now?

DYLAN: Nothing.

KATE: Dylan you got to understand. I'm just trying to protect you. You're a bit inexperienced when it comes to girls. She's not the kind of person you want as a friend.

DYLAN: I'm ok. I've got to finish off some coursework.

KATE: Yes well I have to go to class too you know. PAUSES. SLYLY. Hold on. Oh no. I think I forgot my homework. Dylan can I borrow your phone to text my Mum? I'm out of credit.

DYLAN: UNWILLINGLY. Ummm ok. HANDS HER THE PHONE. SHE PUNCHES A MESSAGE INTO IT THEN HANDS IT BACK.

KATE: That's everything taken care of. Thanks. SHE FLOUNCES OFF. ENTER MICHAEL.

MICHAEL: Watch out mate. Kate wouldn't notice you if you were on fire unless she wanted something.

DYLAN: But she was your girlfriend.

MICHAEL: And Hitler ran Germany once. Hey geek. Have you done your biology? Let me copy it?

DYLAN: What's going on?

MICHAEL: What do you mean?

DYLAN: Well here you are all of a sudden wanting to be mates. And just now Kate was here carrying on like she's like my best friend and she hardly ever talks to me.

MICHAEL: I wouldn't touch Kate with rubber gloves mate. She's poison.

DYLAN: What happened with you and her? Do you want to talk about it?

MICHAEL: Look it was over two weeks ago. What makes you think that I care about what Kate says or does?

DYLAN: It's just I was reading some old posts on your Facebook page last night from people asking if you were okay. I just thought…

MICHAEL: Don't Facebook stalk me you freak. I can't help it if people want to make more of a drama about it than it really is. The only thing that pisses me off is she got to drop me before I could drop her first.

DYLAN: Okay.

MICHAEL: Look I just want to copy your homework. I'm not interested in having a threesome with you and your laptop.

DYLAN: DYLAN'S PHONE BUZZES. Hang on. READS. HE LOOKS TOTALLY GUTTED. That sucks.

MICHAEL: What is it?

DYLAN: READS. 'Not interested in anything you think, say or do. You're just a sad loser. Keep away from me.'

MICHAEL: Ouch. Who did you piss off?

DYLAN: It's from Emma! Why would she say that to me? I gotta go talk to her.

MICHAEL: You're joking right?

DYLAN: Why would I be joking? We were friends a minute ago. Someone must have said something to her.

MICHAEL: Or maybe she's just not interested. Do you think you got overexcited because a girl was actually talking to you? She's just saying how it is.

DYLAN: I can't believe she'd do that. We gotta talk this through.

MICHAEL: Talk it through? Don't you have any self-respect?

DYLAN: You can talk.

MICHAEL: Don't put you and me in the same boat mate. Face it. She was never going to be interested in you.

DYLAN: Shut up. I gotta find out what's going on. HE STARTS TO TEXT. MICHAEL GRABS HIS ARM.

MICHAEL: You're letting her play you. Kate was telling some of her friends earlier that Emma had a bad rep at her old school.

DYLAN: How would she know for sure? It's only just stories.

MICHAEL: Give me her number then and I'll text her. DYLAN HESITATES THEN SHOWS MICHAEL THE NUMBER. MICHAEL SENDS A MESSAGE OFF QUICKLY.

DYLAN: What did you write?

MICHAEL: I just said 'What is up with you and Dylan?' A PAUSE AS THEY WAIT TO SEE IF THERE'S A REPLY. Nothing. Looks like she's ignoring us. THE PHONE BEEPS.

DYLAN: What is it?

MICHAEL: 'Leave me alone'.

DYLAN: Is that all?

MICHAEL: So maybe Kate's right. She's a player.

DYLAN: This sucks.

* * * * *

KATE SEES EMMA LOOKING MISERABLE AND GOES UP TO HER.

KATE: Hey, what's your star sign?

EMMA: What? Sagittarius. Why?

KATE: That's a shame. Oh well.

EMMA: What do you mean?

KATE: I'm a Scorpio. Look it up.

EMMA: I don't follow star signs much.

KATE: No I bet you don't.

EMMA: It's just not my thing.

KATE: Hey, don't take it personally, though I guess you can't help it can you?

EMMA: I don't know what I should take personally. I don't seem to be able to judge anything about anyone.

KATE: You seemed to be getting on well with Dylan.

EMMA: He's the worst of the lot. Pretending to be a nice guy. Maybe not the coolest but you know, friendly, someone I could talk to. And then he sent me this. SHE SHOWS KATE A TEXT MESSAGE ON HER PHONE.

KATE: Feral.

EMMA: I mean if it was something I had said or did, even by accident, I could maybe understand it but I've done nothing.

KATE: Well to be honest you made a bad call even talking to Dylan in the first place. Maybe that was your problem. He is a bit of a freak.

EMMA: How am I supposed to know these things? He seemed okay. I feel like I've screwed up and it's only my second day.

KATE: Don't give up so easy. I reckon Michael's got the hots for you.

EMMA: That's not funny.

KATE: Whatever. Gotta go. SHE EXITS. EMMA WATCHES HER GO THEN GETS UP SLOWLY AND EXITS IN THE OPPOSITE DIRECTION.

* * * * *

DYLAN IS IN HIS BEDROOM TYPING ON THE COMPUTER.

VOICE OF MUM: Dylan, are you going to stay up in your room all night? Why don't you come down and watch Game of Thrones with us?

DYLAN: CALLS. I can stream it later. I'm busy.

VOICE OF MUM: You're always busy.

DYLAN: And when I'm watching tele you say I should be doing my homework.

VOICE OF MUM: As long as you're not...

DYLAN AND MUM: …wasting time on the computer.

DYLAN: Only if you call homework a waste of time. MUTTERS. Which it probably is. HE WORKS INTENTLY ON HIS COMPUTER.

EMMA IS IN HER ROOM WHEN HER PHONE RINGS.

EMMA: Hi Maddy.

VOICE OF MADDY: Hi Ems.

EMMA: Oh it's so good to hear your voice.

VOICE OF MADDY: You too. Look, just wondering if you had checked Facebook. You've been tagged in a really weird post.

EMMA: Hang on I'll check it out now. SHE CHECKS FACEBOOK ON HER PHONE. HER FACE SCREWS UP. Oh that is just pathetic. Don't worry. It's just this loser guy at my new school. I barely know him but he's got serious issues.

VOICE OF MADDY: Yeah but why has it got so many likes?

EMMA: Dunno. He probably belongs to some sicko group who just click like on anything like this. Look, he's just showing the world what a sad life he must have. Nobody would take stuff like that seriously. I've got more important things to worry about.

* * * * *

DYLAN'S PHONE RINGS. THERE IS A CLEAR CHANGE IN HIS BOY LANGUAGE AS HE ANSWERS.

DYLAN: Harry here. Hey Brodie. This is a surprise. No, no it's not a bad time. How are things in L.A.? Oh my post? Yeah just a share from a mate of mine who is still in school over here. He was having problems with some girl who was messing with him. I just felt for him you know. You have to be so careful, don't you babe? Look I've got to meet a few mates in a bit and need to shower and get ready. I'll chat to you online soon.

SOMEBODY ELSE

DYLAN: I close my eyes and try to see
A totally different and confident me
Someone with real status, somebody they cannot ignore
But what's the point? It's just a game
I open my eyes and things all are the same
There's no point pretending, things all stay the same as before
But why live my life with my eyes open wide?
It just blinds the dreams I have hidden inside
When I draw the curtains I'm finally able to be
Somebody else. Somebody else.

I guess you think I'm kind of dumb
Creating the person I'd like to become
And thinking about it I guess that it looks pretty sad
Well you can laugh and say 'who cares?'
What makes my dreams less important than theirs?
Who says that they're right and that what I want is wrong or bad?
Sure others believe that they can have it all
Compared to them all my ambitions are small
I'd settle for just a few moments believing I am

Somebody else. Somebody else.

One day I am gonna show them that I'm not the loser everybody thinks they see
One day people that ignored this lonely guy will suffer and will feel the same as me
One day when the moon is blue and hell has frozen over I won't feel that I need to be
Somebody else. Somebody else. Somebody else. Somebody else.

And if you were me I'd bet you'd wish you were somebody else.

* * * * *

ENTER MICHAEL. KATE ENTERS AND RUNS UP TO HIM.

KATE: So is it true you've been talking to Emma?

MICHAEL: What? Where is this coming from?

KATE: Well you had her number didn't you? How else could you have given it to Dan?

MICHAEL: How did you even know that?

KATE: Well?

MICHAEL: We were just having a talk after footy training and he was asking if I had heard anything about her and I told him about what happened with her and Dylan – hilarious – and how he had given me her number so I could text her to ask what the problem was. We were just having a bit of a laugh about it and then Dan asked if he could have it because she had some notes he needed. So I gave it to him.

KATE: Good move idiot. Rachel found out he had her number.

MICHAEL: So what?

KATE: God you are so stupid.

MICHAEL: I'd forgotten how much I missed being told I was stupid every day by you.

KATE: Emma is so desperate giving out her number to everyone.

MICHAEL: What?

KATE: Well Rachel tweeted it so everyone has it now.

MICHAEL: Well Rachel's the problem then.

KATE: She's not the one hitting on everyone's boyfriend.

MICHAEL: You're sick sometimes Kate you know that?

KATE: So you're defending her? No surprise there.

MICHAEL: Oh for God's sake. KATE'S MOBILE BEEPS. SHE READS THE TEXT SHE HAS RECEIVED.

KATE: I have to talk to Rachel. Try not to make a fool of yourself. SHE EXITS. MICHAEL STANDS THERE EXASPERATED.

EMMA ENTERS. SHE IS STARING AT HER PHONE AND WALKS PAST HIM.

MICHAEL: Don't say hello then.

EMMA: Sorry. SHE WAVES HER PHONE IN THE AIR DISTRACTEDLY.

MICHAEL: What's up?

EMMA: Dunno. Things must have changed since yesterday. Suddenly I am getting all these friend requests from people here at school. Most of them I haven't even talked to yet.

MICHAEL: Well it doesn't mean anything. Some people collect friends on Facebook and never even talk to them or know who they are. Not my thing.

EMMA: Mine either usually but maybe it's the way to settle in here more quickly.

MICHAEL: You seem happier than yesterday.

EMMA: Yeah well I have to make the most of it don't I? I had a long chat to my best friend back home last night and it sort of put things in perspective.

MICHAEL: Okay cool. But look, just be careful about who you talk to okay?

EMMA: If you mean that Dylan kid don't worry. I know exactly what a freak he is. You should have seen what he posted on last night about me. Sad. Still you know. Bound to make some mistakes.

MICHAEL: Yeah.

EMMA: Yeah well umm okay. Thanks. See ya. SHE EXITS.

MICHAEL: Yeah. Later. DYLAN ENTERS.

DYLAN: What did she want?

MICHAEL: Jealous?

DYLAN: As if.

MICHAEL: Look, not that I care how much of a fool you make of yourself, but advertising what a massive fail you had with Emma on Facebook last night... Well it's not going to do you any favours.

DYLAN: She had it coming. I need to let my friends know what kind of person she is.

MICHAEL: Your friends? Right.

DYLAN: Looks like we both have been burnt eh?

MICHAEL: What?

DYLAN: Girls.

MICHAEL: Dude, mention you and me in the same sentence like that again and I'm going to have to punch you in the face.

DYLAN: I was just saying...

MICHAEL: Just shut your face. HE WALKS OFF.

DYLAN: Okay…

* * * * *

EMMA IS CHATTING TO MADDY.

EMMA: …so yeah. Much better today. Not exactly huge fun great time but I was kind of left alone most of the time which for the moment suits me just fine.

VOICE OF MADDY: Being left alone doesn't sound like you.

EMMA: Look I know but I reckon I'll just keep quiet for a while and ease myself into things. Can't expect to make friends straight away right?

VOICE OF MADDY: Maybe after things have settled you can talk to your parents about coming back here, at least to finish the year. I'm sure you could stay at my place. EMMA'S PHONE BEEPS.

EMMA: Thanks Mads. Maybe. But you know what my Dad is like. Hang on. SHE LOOKS AT THE PHONE, ROLLS HER EYES AND SIGHS.

VOICE OF MADDY: What is it?

EMMA: Just a text. READS. 'I'm watching you'. It's from a blocked number.

VOICE OF MADDY: That's scary. Go and tell your Mum and Dad.

EMMA: No. Not going to give whoever it is the satisfaction of thinking I'm worried.

MADDY: What if it's like some serious stalker or pedo or something?

EMMA: I think you have watched Scream too many times. No seriously Mads. It's okay.

MADDY: Promise you'll do something about it if you get any more.

EMMA: I promise.

MADDY: I bet it's that guy who posted about you last night. The one you told me about.

EMMA: Who? Dylan? Maybe. Pathetic if it is. Pathetic anyway. Every time I saw him at school today he just scuttled away in the opposite direction. He's so primary school. Anyway gotta go. I'm starving. Chat later.

MADDY: Bye Ems.

*****

DYLAN ENTERS AND SEES EMMA. HE TURNS TO LEAVE BUT SHE CALLS HIM.

EMMA: Hey.

DYLAN: What?

EMMA: Was that you calling me last night?

DYLAN: I don't know what you're talking about.

EMMA: Well just stop.

DYLAN: I haven't done anything. You're the one who started it.

EMMA: Started what? I didn't start anything.

DYLAN: You calling me a loser not starting anything?

EMMA: Well what was I supposed to do? I'm not going to put up with you being a freak.

DYLAN: And I thought you might have been different to everyone else. Nope, you are just like the rest. It didn't take you long to fit right in did it?

EMMA: Leave me alone. Get it. Just pretend I don't exist.

DYLAN: Suits me. EMMA EXITS. KATE ENTERS

KATE: Hey some of the girls were just talking about your girlfriend Emma. You better watch out Dylan. Sounds like you're just one on a long list.

DYLAN: She's not my girlfriend Kate. She's not any kind of friend. You were right about her.

KATE: Not friends eh? Prove it.

DYLAN: How?

KATE: Let me have a look at your phone?

DYLAN: Why?

KATE: Just let me have a look for a sec. HE HANDS HER HIS PHONE. SHE FLICKS THROUGH IT. Ah ha. If she's not your friend why is she here in your contacts? I bet you swap little love messages all night.

DYLAN: We're not friends. I've never sent her a text in my life. You can delete it if you don't believe me.

KATE: Not my problem who you're friends with. SHE FIDDLES WITH THE PHONE.

DYLAN: What are you doing? Give me my phone back.

KATE: Wait a sec. SHE FINISHES.

DYLAN: What are you doing?

KATE: Nothing. See for yourself. SHE HANDS IT BACK.

DYLAN: LOOKING AT IT. You deleted all my history.

KATE: Did I? Whoops sorry. I just wanted to see if you were telling the truth about you and Emma. Guess you're not lovers after all. Smart choice. Bye Dylan. SHE EXITS.

DYLAN: What was all that about? HE EXITS.

MICHAEL SEES EMMA IN THE SCHOOL YARD.

MICHAEL: Hey.

EMMA: FLATLY. Hi.

MICHAEL: Someone's in a bad mood today.

EMMA: Had a bad night.

MICHAEL: How come?

EMMA: I was getting these texts. The caller was blocked so I couldn't tell who from but they kept coming even at 4 in the morning.

MICHAEL: What were they saying?

EMMA: You don't want to know.

MICHAEL: Yes I do.

EMMA: It started off just stupid stuff like 'I can see you' and stuff like that but as it got later the messages started to get really sick.

MICHAEL: Why didn't you tell someone?

EMMA: I was going to tell my folks before school but Dad was all stressed about his new job and Mum was in one of her 'don't bother me' moods. Anyway if I just ignore it whoever is sending them will probably get bored and stop.

MICHAEL: Probably.

EMMA: What is it about this place? Everyone is so down on me. I can't talk to anyone.

MICHAEL: You're talking to me.

EMMA: You know what I mean.

MICHAEL: You can't expect to just turn up here and be the most popular girl in the school.

EMMA: I don't expect anything like that. But people everywhere seem to have made their mind up about me before I've even met them.

MICHAEL: Hey I was only saying…

EMMA: I'm sick of being treated like a freak. What's the point of even trying to make any friends here? KATE ENTERS.

KATE: Michael. Can I talk to you for a minute? ARCHLY. Oh hi Emma.

MICHAEL: I'm busy.

KATE: No you really need to hear this.

MICHAEL: What is it?

KATE: It's… private.

EMMA: TO MICHAEL. Don't let me stop you. SHE EXITS.

MICHAEL: Well?

KATE: I was just rescuing you. After all the stories going around at the moment you don't want to be seen with her.

MICHAEL: I think I can figure out who I can talk to without your help.

58

KATE: Suit yourself. SHE AND MICHAEL EXIT IN DIFFERENT DIRECTIONS.

* * * * *

EMMA IS TALKING TO MADDY ON HER MOBILE.

VOICE OF MADDY: Why haven't you told anyone?

EMMA: I'm telling you.

VOICE OF MADDY: That's not enough. If it's as bad as you say you've got to make them stop somehow.

EMMA: But how? Besides I am sure that if I tell my parents now they will go straight to school and that will only end up making it worse.

VOICE OF MADDY: Can it be worse?

EMMA: It doesn't seem so bad after talking to you.

VOICE OF MADDY: I'm always here for you Ems.

EMMA: I'll be okay. Just have to give it time right?

VOICE OF MADDY: Yeah. When they get to know you they'll see what a good person you are.

EMMA: Thanks Maddy.

VOICE OF MADDY: Now onto more important stuff. Any cute guys?

EMMA: Well funny enough the guys here are much more friendly than the girls - apart from that one loser I told you about.

VOICE OF MADDY: Anyone in particular?

EMMA: Not really. Well there was this one guy who I was talking to on the way home today. He was really nice.

VOICE OF MADDY: Ooh tell me more.

EMMA: Well his name is Dave... No hang on. Dan. Something like that. He kind of had this hipster vibe but not, you know, too much.

VOICE OF MADDY: What does he... Oh hang on... Sorry Ems have to go. Mum is yelling to come and eat. We can talk again after dinner if you want?

EMMA: Cool. See you Maddy. Love you.

MADDY: Love you too. Bye.

EMMA PHONE BEEPS. SHE CHECKS IT, STIFFENS THEN SCREAMS.

EMMA: I hate this place!

*****

EMMA IS SITTING ALONE. MICHAEL ENTERS.

MICHAEL: What are you doing here today?

EMMA: Well it's a school day isn't it? I have to come here even if everyone here hates me.

MICHAEL: But I heard you had… Well just that you wouldn't be here today?

EMMA: Heard what? And who did you hear it from?

MICHAEL: Something on Twitter. I reckon you were trending more than Justin Beiber.

EMMA: About what?

MICHAEL: Doesn't matter.

EMMA: You can't just say that. What is it?

MICHAEL: Did you really get with every guy in the football team back at your old school at their end of season party?

EMMA: What? No! What?

MICHAEL: Didn't think it was true.

EMMA: Why would people say that? It's not true. Why can't people leave me alone? SHE STARTS TO CRY.

MICHAEL: Oh no. I mean umm. Look don't worry about it. HE TRIES TO COMFORT HER AWKWARDLY. SHE RELAXES FOR A MOMENT THEN STIFFENS AND BREAKS AWAY.

EMMA: I hate this place. SHE EXITS. MICHAEL STANDS THERE CONFLICTED. ENTER KATE.

KATE: Have you spoken to Dan today?

MICHAEL: Haven't seen him. Why?

KATE: Rachael dumped him. That's why.

MICHAEL: Huh. Didn't see that coming. Why would she do that?

KATE: Someone Instagrammed a photo to Rachel last night of him walking home with Emma after school. Evidently she took him back to her place. What a skank.

MICHAEL: Did she actually ask him about it?

KATE: Everyone was talking about it. She was humiliated so she just texted him and told him to throw himself under a train and won't talk to him at all. That's why I wanted to know if you had talked to him.

MICHAEL: Emma just doesn't seem the type.

KATE: You still got the hots for her? She's making a fool of you Mike. Everyone is starting to notice. She puts out for every other guy she lays eyes on and you follow her around like a puppy. What do you think your mates are saying about that?

MICHAEL: I'm not buying that.

KATE: Don't you even read the posts. People are laughing at you.

MICHAEL: Bull.

KATE: Just looking out for you Mike. I still care what people say about you, you know.

MICHAEL: But it's not true. I'm not.

KATE: Of course you're not. Poor Mike. Used to be the big man and now some little nobody from the country is making him a laughing stock.

MICHAEL: I'm not a goddamned laughing stock.

KATE: The only one who treats her nicely is the only one who's not getting any. SHE MOVES IN AND GIVES HIM A HUG. Just try to not let her make a fool of you. Well more of a fool than your mates say you are already. EXIT KATE.

GOT TO STOP

MICHAEL: This is crazy. What are people saying? I have got to go and make it stop now. Where is she?

I gotta stop the rot, the rot that set in back when I was dumped
When I was dumped it really hit me hard but time to get back up
And show them I'm as cool as I have ever been but maybe even tougher
Than I was before I let them see that I could care.

Even when I cared I was the guy in charge or that was how it seemed to all my mates until she turned around and dropped me. When she dropped me things went off the rails a little, maybe I made a bad call because instead of being cool I showed that I was hurt.

But that was then and this is now and no-one makes a fool of Michael. No-one's gonna laugh at me behind my back or say that I am being dumb or lost the plot so time for them to all shut up. And if that crazy chick is putting out then what is wrong with me?
So if everyone was talking time for them to shut the hell up.

Everyone is talking. Everyone is laughing at me. All my mates are laughing. This has got to stop now.

EMMA IS SITTING ALONE. MICHAEL COMES UP TO HER.

MICHAEL: Hiding behind the old gym huh. Makes sense.

EMMA: What?

MICHAEL: Nothing. Just that no-one ever hangs around this part of the school.

EMMA: That's why I'm here. I just want to be left alone.

MICHAEL: You sure you don't want company?

EMMA: I'm not sure about anything anymore.

MICHAEL: I'm just trying to be nice to you. Give you a chance to be nice to me.

EMMA: What are you talking about?

MICHAEL: Come on. I heard about you and Dan.

EMMA: Who's Dan?

MICHAEL: Doesn't matter. DRAGS HER TO HER FEET. How about you just be nice and friendly. SHE IS HORRIFIED.

EMMA: Leave me alone!!!

MICHAEL: Stop playing games. I'm not going to let you make me look like a loser in front of all my friends. HE TRIES TO KISS HER. SHE SCREAMS, BREAKS FREE AND RUNS AWAY. MICHAEL SNAPS INTO FOCUS. Oh no. I'm sorry. CALLING AFTER HER. I'm sorry! It was just a bad joke. I didn't mean it. Emma! It was just a joke. HE RUNS OUT AFTER HER.

ENTER KATE. EMMA PRACTICALLY COLLIDES WITH HER.

KATE: What's wrong?

EMMA: I can't come back to this place. It's insane. The teachers don't seem to notice. I can't tell my parents. What am I supposed to do? Why is everything so...?

KATE: Calm down. What happened?

EMMA: I can't do this. SHE EXITS. ENTER MICHAEL.

KATE: What's wrong with Emma?

MICHAEL: She's gone crazy. I mean... Oh God. This is all wrong. HE GOES TO RUN AFTER HER BUT KATE GRABS HIM.

KATE: Calm down. Let her go. She's not worth it.

MICHAEL: You don't understand. I've really stuffed up.

KATE: Why?

MICHAEL: This is your fault Kate. It never would have happened if you hadn't put me up to it.

KATE: I haven't put you up to anything.

MICHAEL: I've been such an idiot.

KATE: Mike whatever it is it's not your fault. She's been after you ever since she came here, you and every other guy. She's trouble. Just keep away from her.

MICHAEL: Too late. Too late. ENTER DYLAN.

DYLAN: Did you see Emma just then?

KATE: Can't you ever tell when you are not wanted?

DYLAN: No this is weird. She has, like, lost it. She was screaming and crying. When someone went up to find out what was wrong she just totally freaked and ran out of the school grounds.

MICHAEL: Oh hell. What do you think she's going to do?

KATE: Michael will you please just chill. Maybe she'll take herself to another school now or something. Good riddance I say.

DYLAN: Do you think we should tell someone?

KATE: Like who? And anyway what would it sound like coming from you. Just forget about it. KATE LEADS MICHAEL OFF. DYLAN STANDS NOT KNOWING WHAT TO DO.

* * * * *

EMMA IS ALONE IN HER ROOM TALKING ON HER MOBILE.

VOICE OF MADDY: Hi this is Maddy. Busy, so leave a message. I'll call you soon as I can. Bye.

EMMA: Maddy. Maddy please pick up. I can't stand it. There's no-one home. I'm all alone. It's all too hard. It's all too hopeless. DROPPING THE PHONE. I just can't do this anymore.

EASY WAY OUT

EMMA: I used to be okay
I used to get on well with everyone
Until I came here
But things are different now
It's like a nightmare when you don't wake up
But one thing is clear
I don't belong here and I never will
And there's no-one who understands

How do you get out when there's no easy way out?
Where do you go to when you have nowhere to go?
How do you get out when there's no easy way out?
And who can you turn to?

I'm angry and I'm sad
I'm lonely, frightened, lost
I'm going mad

How do you get out when there's no easy way out?
Where do you go to when you have nowhere to go?
How do you get out when there's no easy way out?
And who can you turn to?
I've no-one to turn to
Nothing. No-one.

* * * * *

THERE IS THE SOUND OF POLICE SIRENS. MICHAEL AND DYLAN ARE SITTING OUTSIDE THE PRINCIPAL'S OFFICE. MICHAEL LOOKS SICK. ENTER KATE.

KATE: What's this about? Why have they called us up? Why are there police here?

MICHAEL: I'm a goner. I'm going to be expelled. I'm going to jail.

KATE: Do you think she snaked on you?

DYLAN: Who snaked on who? What are you talking about?

KATE: Mike it wasn't your fault. She brought that on herself.

MICHAEL: Did she? Did she really?

KATE: People know you're a good guy. They won't listen to her.

DYLAN: What do they want to talk to me for?

THEY ALL LOOK UP AS A DOOR OPENS AND MOVE TO ISOLATED SPOTS ON THE STAGE.

KATE: Yes I knew her a bit but I didn't talk to her much. She didn't really hang around with any of my friends. She was more interested in hanging around with guys. Look, what's going on? Has something happened to her? Why am I being asked questions by the police? I haven't done anything. Can I go now?

MICHAEL: I talked to her a couple of times but that's about all. She was a bit up herself. Kept to herself a fair bit. If you want to find out about people picking on her ask Kate. She was leading the pack against her. And why aren't you asking Emma these questions anyway? Where is she?

KATE: I didn't really even care what she did. Yeah people were talking about all this bad stuff she did at her old school but so what? People talk. If you really want to know about her ask Dylan. He was obsessed with her. Practically stalked her. Is that why she isn't at school today?

DYLAN: No I don't know what happened to Emma. And I don't know why you're asking me why I was picking on her. She started it. She pretended to be my friend then turned on me for no reason. No I didn't send her abusive text messages. I never sent her any messages after she told me to get lost. I don't know why that message on her phone is from me. I never sent it. Hang on. Ask Kate. She used my phone. She must have sent them. I bet it was her. Is Emma okay?

KATE: He's lying. Why would I do something like that? He was the one obsessing about her all the time. You can see it on his Facebook. He's just desperate and trying to push the blame away.

DYLAN: Yes I know I posted that but she started it. Who's Harry? I don't know anyone called Harry? Well yeah but that's just a bit of fun. How did you know I had a Facebook account for Harry? Well I didn't think anyone would take what he said seriously. I mean he was just made up. Is there a law against that? Oh there is? Why does it matter? This is so not fair. And what's happened to Emma?

DON'T ASK ME

DYLAN: You know better than me what the hell is going on
You know better than me people who became involved
You know better than me what her movements were last night
You know better than me who she has been talking to
You know better than me what this whole thing is about
So don't ask me I don't know anything
Don't ask me, find someone else
Seems to me you know what's going on
So I'm telling you don't ask me

KATE: Look I wasn't involved, go and ask the other kids
Look I wasn't involved, you should talk to someone else
Look I wasn't involved, we were just mucking around
Look I wasn't involved, I just said what I'd been told
Look I wasn't involved, this is all a big mistake
So don't ask me I don't know anything
Don't ask me, find someone else
Seems to me you know what's going on
So I'm telling you don't ask me

DYLAN, MICHAEL AND KATE: How did you know that?
Who told you?
I didn't say that? How come you
Are asking me all these crazy questions?
Don't ask me I don't know anything
Don't ask me, find someone else
Seems to me you know what's going on
So I'm telling you don't ask me

DYLAN: Look I wasn't involved
We were mucking around
This is all a mistake.

OUTSIDE THE OFFICE. MICHAEL IS SITTING ALONE. KATE ENTERS.

MICHAEL: Kate. What did you tell them?

KATE: I didn't tell them anything?

MICHAEL: But the cops have called you up twice? What did you do to Emma? You know what people are saying?

KATE: No I don't know what people are saying and I didn't do anything to her. How come I'm the bad one all of a sudden? Everyone was happy to joke about her until this morning and now she's like some tragic victim and it's somehow my fault. I don't think so.

MICHAEL: You can make all the excuses you want Kate. Whatever has happened to Emma it's partly your fault.

KATE: At least I didn't assault her.

MICHAEL: I never would have touched her if you hadn't filled my head with all that crap.

KATE: You say that now. I might have made a few mistakes but everyone else is to blame as well. Come on Mikey. Don't be like that.

MICHAEL: Forget it Kate. I know what you are now. You can't fool me like you used to.

KATE: It's not fair. It wasn't me. It was Dylan. He's the crazy one. HE TURNS AWAY FROM HER. TO HERSELF. What am I supposed to do?

DYLAN ENTERS.

DYLAN: They said to tell you you can go now Kate.

MICHAEL: That'd be right.

KATE: Why is everyone acting as if it's my fault? It's not as if I'm not getting grief too. Can you even imagine what my parents are going to say about me being questioned by the police?

MICHAEL: Suck it in.

SHE TRIES TO THINK OF SOMETHING ELSE TO SAY BUT THEN TURNS AND LEAVES.

MICHAEL: What did they ask you in there?

DYLAN: The police seemed to know everything. Everything I've said and done. It was humiliating. They had a list of every porn site I had ever visited. Imagine what that's gonna be like when my parents see that.

MICHAEL: We're both stuffed mate.

DYLAN: But I didn't even send those texts that were on Emma's phone. And stuff I said online - I didn't start it.

MICHAEL: Doesn't matter. We're gonners.

DYLAN: Why won't they tell us what happened to Emma?
MICHAEL: I don't know.

DYLAN: You don't think…

EMMA COMES UP IN A SPOT.

EMMA: What happened to me? Well that night my head was full of desperate, crazy, dangerous thoughts. I was on the edge about to fall off the cliff when Mum came running into my room. Maddy had got my message and called her. It was such a relief just saying things out loud about how I was feeling, what had been happening - the texts, the stuff that had been on Facebook, the filthy emails that had been circulated. My parents said after all this that I could go back to my old school but the head teacher talked us into staying. He promised things would be different. What made things a bit easier was that I didn't have to deal with Kate any more as her parents pulled her out and sent her to some private girls' school. The whole business won't go away overnight but I'll survive. And as for the people at school that almost ruined my life. Well I should say I hope they're all wiser and better now but honestly I just hope their lives are all stuffed up forever.

CONNECTED (reprise)

EMMA: If you've read something online well then it must be true

DYLAN: If someone heard it somewhere then it must be true

KATE: If it is on a website then it must be true

MICHAEL: If you think that perhaps maybe then it must be true

TOGETHER: If it was texted to you then it must be true
If everybody's Tweeting it, it must be true
If it's up on someone's Facebook then it must be true
If you believe it there's no doubt it must be true

TOGETHER: You've got to be connected
You've got to know who's in and who is out
You've got to stay connected
The only way to know what life's about
It don't take much to have it
Or to have it ripped away
Coz that's what's needed to be popular…

FIN

OTHER TITLES AVAILABLE FROM ORiGiN™ THEATRICAL

FEEDEM FIGHTERS
Dorian Mode

A fattening new Aussie Comedy all about food!

Daryl Lucas is a fat, happily married soft-drink salesman living on the NSW Central Coast until the day he walks in on his cheating cougar wife and her young Pilates instructor. While he plots to divorce her, she arranges for Daryl to be kidnapped by a group of disparate lunatics calling themselves Feedem Fighters. Inspired by shows like *Extreme Makeover* and *The Biggest Loser*, these calorie terrorists kidnap fatties and keep them captive in a soundproof room for three months, forcing them to lose weight. Can Daryl convince them he's only being held so his wife can drain his accounts and run off with her Pilates instructor? You'll laugh so much you'll lose two kilos!

"As comedies go, Feedem Fighters couldn't get much more topical. What follows is a rollicking commentary on our nation's love affair with exploit-o-porn reality TV highlighting the ironic dual-success of shows which feature both cooking and dieting. Those who crave farces, but are sick of being forced-fed Ayckbourn and Cooney would find this very satisfying comedy fare."
– *Rose Cooper, Stage Whispers*

Cast: 5 Male & 1 Female
(or 3m and 1f w/- doubling, plus 1m & 1 f voice only)

www.origintheatrical.com.au

OTHER TITLES AVAILABLE FROM ORiGiN™ THEATRICAL

HER HOLINESS
Justin Fleming & Melvyn Morrow

Her Holiness combines humour and drama in dealing with life and death battles and survival in Australia – then and now.

1867 – All Mary MacKillop wanted was to live the dream. But to others (the staunch male hierarchy of the Roman Catholic Church) she was a nightmare. What MacKillop didn't count on was the degree of obstruction that would stand in her way.

2008 – One hundred and forty years after Mary MacKillop another young Australian woman, Anna, goes to Rome with a passionate mission to seek an audience with Pope Benedict XVI to push for the final steps of Mary MacKillop's case to be Australia's first Saint.

She was Australia's Martin Luther. The antipodean Thomas More. Our Joan of Arc. A woman for all seasons.

"A stunning new play. Australian work at its finest."
– Arts Hub

"A confronting, moving and very entertaining piece of theatre"
– Australian Stage

Cast: 6 Female & 11 Male (multiple doubling of roles)
Plus guards, beggar(s), Chief of Police

www.origintheatrical.com.au

Printed by Libri Plureos GmbH in Hamburg, Germany